When Two Hearts Meet

(Your's and Mine)

Peggy Kaplan

When Two Hearts Meet
(Your's and Mine)

Paperback

ISBN: 978-0990389361

Published by; Shoestring Book Publishing.

Copyright 2014
By, Peggy Kaplan
All rights reserved.
Printed in the United States of America.

No part of this book may be reproduced, stored in a retrieval system, or transmitted in any form, electronic, mechanical; or by other means whatsoever, without written permission from the author. Except for the case of brief quotations within reviews and critical articles.

Shoestring Book Publishing accepts no liability for the content of this book, or for the consequences of any actions taken on the basis of the information provided herein. The thoughts expressed in this book are solely the thoughts of the author and not those of Shoestring Book Publishing.

Layout and design by Shoestring Book Publishing
For information address;
shoestringpublishing4u@gmail.com

When Two Hearts Meet

(Your's and Mine)

PEGGY KAPLAN

SHOESTRING BOOK PUBLISHING

Dedication

This book is dedicated to the Holy Spirit for continued inspiration.

My Husband Joe, my Grandchildren James and Julia and my two sons Mike and Dan.

A special thank you to my sister Debby for all her editorial help. And all my special friends for your loving support.

All Bible verses are taken from the New Living Translation.

To believe is having peace in the storms of life.

Table of Contents

Preface viii

You are Love 2

Patti 4

Thinking of Me 6

Brighter Tomorrow 10

What will you give 9

Skating 8

A Walk in the Woods 11

In Prayer 12

Reason 14

Portrait of Jesus 15

Prayer Away 16

My Sister 17

Spring 18

Quietness of my mind 19

The Beginning 20

Another Day 21

When I was Young 22

Waves 24

Bible 25

Jesus Speaks 26

When two Hearts Meet *28*
God is Watching *29*
The Day Jesus Died *30*
To my Brother *31*
Who Will You Choose *32*
Come with Me *33*
Alone *34*
A Neighbors View *35*
Tell them I Love them *36*
Forever and a Day *37*
Sleepless *38*
Listening ⋯ *39*
Sleeping Soundly *40*
Friends *41*
The Crow *42*
Springtime *43*
Comfort in my Bible *44*
Your Love *45*
The Lost *46*
Mercy and Love *48*
My Bible *49*
Dreams *50*
Our Foundation *52*
Your Word *53*

When Lord 54

Heart and Mind 55

Lord Jesus 56

Angel 57

Grace 58

Reflection 59

Father's Love 60

Unanswered Prayer 61

New Beginnings 62

About the Author 66

Preface

The idea of the book came when I was prayed over at Hope in Life Church in Carmel NY and the Pastor said I was going to write a book of poems. I have been writing since a young age but never for other people, so I sat down and decided to write. I want to give some of the proceeds from the book to food pantry's in the churches in my area.

You are Love

Surely you are God
Your word when spoken
caused the earth to be formed.
You spoke life
and it appeared;
 your words are so mighty
that even the stars in the heavens
obey them.

Your Spirit reveals all.

Your hand is mightier
than a whole army.
You raise it
and thousands fall,
our enemies are scattered
like bugs.

*I will praise and thank you always
for the wonderful things you have done.
From generation to generation
your hand has been with us,
your spoken word over us
has given us blessings.*

*Your love
can never be explained.
It is as mysterious as you
why have you chosen a sinful people?
Was my Lord lonely?
I think not.
You are surrounded by love,
because you are love.*

Patti

She screams so loud
I can barely breathe.
That squawking makes me want to leave.
She throws her food everywhere,
she doesn't seem to have a care.

Her language is not fit for all,
she's quite the little fireball.
She's always asking;
"What does dog do?"
If you bark-
she'll meow for you.

She does a dance to
cartoon songs,
expecting you to dance along.

You must be careful what you say
she'll pick it up, in just one day.

She imitates the fire alarm,
she really doesn't mean you harm.
You race around from room to room
before you realize there are no fumes.

The doorbell rings, "hello" is heard,
don't answer the door it's just the bird.

In spite of all she may do
God has given me a blessing who,
fills my life with laughter and cheer
every day of every year.

Thinking of Me

In my trials and tribulations
the Lord is thinking of me.
When I have gone out before Him
and lost my way
He is walking with me.

In prayer,
asking forgiveness
of those who hurt me,
the Lord is hearing me.

When I cannot bring
myself to believe
in all his goodness
He believes in me.

When I am filled with bitterness
He shows me mercy.

He thinks of me day and night.
I am always on this mind,
my Lord reminds me
of all the blessings
He has spoken over me;
how much He loves me.

*I will sing His praises,
I will honor His name
in all I do.
I will speak of Him
to my children's children.
They will know of His unfailing love,
they will know that he is near -
watching and protecting them.*

*They will know I trust Him,
with all my heart.
He is my God, He is their God.
He hears everything they say,
knows everything they do.*

*They will know that the
blood of Jesus is protection,
a sign of pure love.
They will know the Lord
is thinking of them.*

Skating

Swaying side to side.
she moves with grace,
her gloves hug her hands,
a hat warming her head.
She is lost in her own thoughts,
as she skates, using
her God given talent.

What will you give

What have you given today?
A smile, a kind word?
Have you wiped a tear away?
fed the hungry?
Sheltered the homeless?
Given love where it's needed,
or simple a prayer?

When you have nothing to give,
give a prayer,
God will do the rest ...

Brighter Tomorrow

*Sometimes the past joins me for
breakfast, lunch and dinner.
Like an unwelcome guest,
it creeps into my emotions
pulling at them,
screaming
for attention .*

*Memories of long ago
creep up on me,
like a cat stalking its prey.
Remembering love gone by,
dreams untold,
plans thwarted,
promises broken.*

*Then You show up;
with Your mercy,
forgiveness and love.
You rebuke the past,
giving me peace
and the promise of a brighter tomorrow.*

A Walk in the Woods

Walking in the woods,
looking for a quiet spot to write a poem.
Birds are chirping,
daisies grow near a rock.
The sound of cars passing on a nearby road,
leaves rustle under my feet.
The quiet peaceful sounds from a running brook.
I found my poem
in God's creation.

In Prayer

I awaken before dawn,
spending time with You in prayer.
You fill me with your peace
before my day begins.

You speak to me in your word,
giving me guidance for the day ahead,
telling me You are near.

You protect me from the unseen things
that lurk in the darkness.
I am yours,
no harm will come to me.

You build a hedge of protection around me,
holding me in the palm of your hand.
Your light hides me from my enemies.

You have planned my every move,
You know where I am going,
what I will say, before I do.

You are my God:
I have no others.
With You I am never alone,
Your love is all I need.

I will lift my hands to You
and give You all the glory,
You are deserving of unlimited love.

Reason

*You have been so patient with me Lord,
waiting for me to learn from my mistakes,
and know it's You
who gives me my blessings.
My heart is filled with joy
because of Your unfailing love;
you are my salvation.*

Portrait of Jesus

As a child, peace and comfort came to me
from a portrait of Jesus
I held near.
Rips and tears were put together,
using tape for the stitches
it would mend.
Sleepless nights, crying days,
I spoke to Jesus in the
portrait it made.
His sacred heart beat just for me,
as I felt him send comfort, love and peace.

Prayer Away

Does Jesus live in your home?
Dine with you at meals?
Do you hear his voice
when all is quiet?
When you are sad,
do you smile;
knowing that he loves you?
He is just a prayer away.

My Sister

My sister, my friend,
God's gift.
She is my family, she is my blood;
we are created in God's love.
He wrapped her up as a gift for me
to keep for all eternity.
I'm thankful each and everyday
the Lord sent you my way.
My sister, my friend,
will always be
a gift that God has given me.

Spring

***B**irds singing,*
flowers blooming,
spring is upon us.
The deer drink from the
stream of cool water.
The morning dew is
sparkling in the grass.
All is good
in God's creation.

Quietness of my mind

In the quietness of my mind
a thought of You breaks through.
I see You everywhere I look;
in the sun, the clouds,
the stillness of the air.
I feel Your presence surround me,
making all my worries disappear,
making me aware that you are the center
of everything.

The Beginning

The sun began to weep.
All was quiet as the clouds
ran across the sky,-
darkening the area where
Jesus hung on the cross.
The very cross he was on began to weep.

"He is the Lord" they cried out.
No one would listen.
Satan thinks he has won!
Jesus, has just begun.

Another Day

I awake speaking a prayer of Thanksgiving
for another day,
another chance for Gods abounding grace,
another chance to see him in those around me.

We are given many chances to do what is right,
but just one day at a time to accomplish it.
We never know what tomorrow brings;
we need to accomplish so much in a single day.

Another chance to make a difference,
another chance to forgive,
another chance to help those in need.

I am thankful for all the blessings I have.
Because of God, I lack for nothing,
except: maybe another day.

When I was Young

When I was born I could not see
my guardian angel next to me.
Now I know she was near,
this became very clear.

When I was small I could not see
the way that You looked at me.
Your love so real, your grace so strong,
I could not see my life was wrong.

When I grew older,
knowing right from wrong,
I choose a path not of your own.
I took for granted your love for me.
Would be there no matter
who I turned out to be?

As an adult when problems grew,
I finally found my way to You.
I could see it fall into place,
I had not known about Your grace.

It did not matter when I prayed,
You were with me every day.
When I forgot all about You,
You held me even closer still.

My problems have not gone away,
I walk with them every day.
The difference now is, I can see;
Your loving mercy walks with me.

Waves

*I watch as waves rush to the shore,
gathering grains of sand;
dropping them on the oceans floor-
rushing back to claim more.
The waves are decorating the ocean's floor.*

Bible

***B**lessed be the name of our Lord,*
***i**n whom we trust;*
***b**less his word, the Bible,*
***l**et all people bless him*
***e**verywhere.*

Jesus Speaks

He *was getting tired, so he closed his eyes for the last time. I wasn't sure at first but I thought I heard him say,* **"I will see you later"** *then the room filled with a brilliant light, so bright, I had to cover my face. Warmth surrounded me, I tried to look.*
It was then I heard him,
"Heaven is real" *he said* **"I am real.**

Speak to me every day, all day in your words and in your deeds. Do not depend on things of this world to give you lasting
 satisfaction, for they too shall fade away.
Call on my name; it has much power for you!
I will hear you and listen, even if you think I'm not.
You will know through my peace I give you.

Come and visit me in my house, I am always happy to see people gather together in my name.
Give me at least that.

Respect one another. You will live together an eternity. Speak of me often to those who do not know, If they do not listen, move on. I will send someone else at the appointed time.

Do not worry so much what you look like.
Don't live to be perfect.
You will never make the mark.

Perfection is in heaven not on earth.
Your body is a tool; keep it healthy, so you can do
my work. In heaven you will be given a new body.

Worship only me,
I shall be your only God.

Satan has brought things into this world
for you to worship.
They will not bring you salvation.

Do not worry about what others have.
I will give you what you need.
You will never do without.
I have given you many blessings.

Do not concern yourself with who will be
with me for all eternity,
I will make that decision.
You cannot know another person's heart as I do,
just love them and give me the sin."

I felt the tears on my face,
I knew I had not been living as he wanted me to.
The room became dark again.
I wasn't sure but I thought I heard him say
one last time;

"I will see you later."

When two Hearts Meet

When two hearts meet, Yours and mine
I will fall to my knees in adoration.
Peace will fill my very being,
I will be unable to speak.

Nothing else will matter.
In Your eyes I will see
what I knew was always there;
unconditional love
beyond anything I have ever felt.
Words do not need to be spoken
when two hearts meet:
Yours and mine.

God is Watching

What's the answer,
let us see.
I think it starts with you and me.
It's not the color of our skin,
God created us
the same within.
Though some may have a harder time
God is there, he is divine.
He didn't say "I am here for you
but not for those
YOU think aren't true".

On judgment day you will see,
He will judge both you and me.
He will not look at what he sees
our color, race, or glamour be.

No! he will look into your heart
and see what's written there.
So be careful now,
at what you do;
God, for sure, is watching you.

The Day Jesus Died

*The forest watched,
the wind whispered,
the sun sang.
The ocean called
to the wailing moon,
flowers withered.
Trees bowed,
the words cried;
the day Jesus died.*

To my Brother

*It's been a year ago today,
that you went so far away,
leaving us with memories
in our hearts for us to grieve.
But we know deep down inside
that you are living now with God;
and one day soon we will be
together again as family.*

Who Will You Choose

God is the creator of all things.
We are given free will
to choose right from wrong.
Some of our choosing's are foolish ones.

God understands our weakness,
he forgives us when we sin no more.

Jesus is the one who hears your cries;
who died for you so that you might
live for all eternity with him.
He promises to always be there.
He does not lie.
He is the same today as yesterday.
His promises hold true for everyone
who accepts him.

Have you accepted him?
The evil one wants to destroy
and kill you for all eternity.
God wants to love you;
who will you choose?

Come with Me
(New Year's Eve with Jesus)

Come with me.
I will take you on a journey,
a place of inspiration,
a place where you can rest in my presence.
I will show you what I have planned for you,
where your dreams come to life,
no more waiting.
Come with me; I will
bring you into the New Year
full of my peace, love and gentleness.
You will see me at every turn,
come with me;
leave behind the old,
we will ring in the new, together.

Alone

A *single tear on her cheek;*
I wondered why she dropped it.
I said lord, ***"You know what's wrong,***
touch her, make her happy."

The clouds moved quickly.
The sun shone through.
Its warmth enveloped her.
Slowly she looked up.

The corner of her mouth rose to meet the sun;
"Ah, there you have it!", *I said to myself.*
The son has dried up her tear.
I smiled.
Thank you, Lord, for an answered prayer.

A Neighbors View

A man and his dog played in the yard,
stopping only for hugs,
tears well up in his eyes.
Then the car ride, the dog so happy.

Later, upon returning, he is alone,
tears running down his face.
My heart breaks to see him cry;
losing his friend is hard on him,

I didn't ask.
I never knew.
Give him your peace, Lord,
fill his emptiness with your love.

Tell them I Love them

*I want to write a poem that will touch
the hearts of the hurting ...
one that will move the hearts of the unbelievers -
to reach out for the Lord.*

*His words, spoken through me,
to bring comfort to the hurting.*

*But, the words will not come, Lord.
I struggle with them day and night;
I do not hear them in my heart,
Your Holy Spirit is quiet.*

*Deep within me, no words, no movement,
Where are the words to brighten up a dreary day?
To bring a smile to a crying child, or,
just to let me know you are near.
Then I hear You in the quietness of my room.*

*"Tell them I love them." you softly say;
"Just tell them I love them."*

Forever and a Day

*Fill me with your patience,
Your all-consuming love.
Fill me with your mercy,
Your peace from above.*

*Show me You are listening
to every word I say,
show me You are there,
with me, every day.*

*I know I don't deserve You,
or the gentle way you say,
"My child; I will love You
forever and a day."*

*I bow my head before You,
I give You all my praise,
I worship and adore you,
forever and a day.*

Sleepless

When I cannot sleep
I think of You!
I see You as my Lord,
sitting by my side
telling me stories
of old.

I imagine I am walking with You,
hearing Your words teach me,
I soak them up
as a dry sponge soaks up
water.
Your living words
bring me peace,
as I close my eyes to sleep.

Listening ...

*In the quietness of my room,
I listen for Your voice.
Sometimes it is so quiet,
I wonder if You're there ...*

*Suddenly, I am aware
of the faint cry of a child
playing outside.*

*It is then,
   I **know** You are near.*

Sleeping Soundly

Snuggled up, all warm in bed,
visions and dreams
roll round my head.
No tossing and turning for me tonight,
I'm sleeping soundly, in Gods' sight.

Friends

*Friends come and go throughout your life,
but the friends Jesus gives you remain forever.
You may not see them every day or speak often,
but they are always there in spirit and love.*

*These friends, who remain by your side
through all the bad times,
cry when you cry, laugh at your jokes
when no one else finds them funny.
They are your sisters in Christ,
share the same heavenly father,
and are the ones God gave you
to let you know
how much he loves you.*

The Crow

She sits.

The top branches
bending lightly under her weight.

She calls to her friends,
gathering them to
eat the freshly scattered bread.

God provides for all his creation.

Written after feeding the birds in my yard.

Springtime

Flowers blooming
birds singing,
plucking worms from
the soft earth.
all of God's creation
is full of life.

Written while I watched a bird tugging at a worm

Comfort in my Bible

*I find comfort in my Bible,
the words God has spoken
bring life to me.*

*My Bible comforts me when sad,
brings hope when I'm in despair.*

*His words are a constant reminder
of His love.*

Your Love

You watch over your loved ones
keeping them safe.
You rain down your blessing
reminding them of who You are.

You will never leave your loved ones,
Your promises are forever,
Your spirit is with us,
giving us wisdom
all day long.

We wait in prayer for Your instructions,
we go where You send us ...
knowing Your spirit is guiding and protecting.
Praise be to you, Almighty God,
for you are deserving of all our love.

The Lost

I ride around throughout the day
in search of what I'll find,
"the lost", My Lord, are everywhere,
they're not that hard to find.

I see them in the streets, My Lord,
in the corners of the shops,
I even see them in the church
asleep in their familiar spots.

I believe in all your promises,
your love beyond compare,
yet deep inside my soul, there are
some things that bring despair.

I have a lack of patience
for the things I cannot see,
though I know you'll take care of them,
it brings anger to me.

"The lost" are also animals ...
Like dogs, and cats, and more.
They wander all throughout the streets,
seek shelter from a storm.

It breaks my beating heart to hear
of what these sinners do;
like, leaving their poor pets alone
with no shelter, love or food.

The elements beat down on them,
they have nowhere to go;
the cars are moving fast
their hearts are hurting so.

Lord, bring them to a safer place
where words of comfort live,
don't let me give up hope I ask,
please, help me to forgive.

Written when someone abandon a dog in a cage on the side of the road in the dead of winter.

Mercy and Love

You suffered for us,
when we were undeserving
of Your love.
Yet, You gave up your life for us,
because You loved us so.

The father gave You to us
to be our savior,
You shed your blood upon the cross.
A death beyond comprehension.

In Your mercy and love,
You suffered and died for us.
Your love is everlasting,
Your mercy undeniable,
You are the Lord of All.

My Bible

My Bible
is the word of God.
Given to me so I may know Him.
It is His law, His guidance, His living word.
The word of God brings comfort,
joy to the heavy-hearted,
faith to the hurting.

God's word is alive in me.

Dreams

Dreams were not created on earth,
without first being created in heaven.
Reach your hands to the heavens
and pull down your dream.
Believe in the dream
God put in your heart.

It's a seed. Water it, and it will grow.
The Lord will cultivate it with a touch of His hand.
Believe in the dream He has planted in your heart.
He gave it to you, alone.

In the morning, when you place
your feet on the ground,
He will be there beside you.

In the evening, thank the Lord
for his guidance.
Just remind Him, oh so gently,

It's a dream that You placed in my heart,
It's a dream I will water and watch grow,
It's a dream that You gave me so long ago.

When my life is done, I will lift up my hands
and give You back my dream!

So You can place it in another's heart, where
it will be a seed for them to water and grow.
You will cultivate it with your hands.

Then, they will believe in the dream
that You planted in their hearts
so long ago.

Our Foundation

A tree with no roots withers and dies.
A home with no foundation
crumbles and falls.

A bird with a broken wing
cannot fly.

Without God,
we have no roots, no foundation,
we are just like the bird with a broken wing.

With God,
we can soar high above the rest,
we will not crumble and fall,
because He is our foundation.

Your Word

*T**he word of God brings comfort to my soul.*
It brings comfort to the weary
and feeds our hearts with hope.
The Word of God is eternal;
  it changes us.

When Lord

Lord, sometimes it's hard to see You at work in my life,
problems are all around me.
I try to keep an open heart and believe
You are working.

I have eyes to see and ears to hear,
sometimes they are blinded and deafened by
disbelief.
my heart is so broken by evils of this world.
I find myself asking You,
Lord, when are You coming?

I get caught up in grief, sorrow swallows me up
when are You coming Lord?
when will the suffering end?
the pain, the evil? When Lord, when?
but I will stand firm in my faith.

I will give You praise and thanks for all
the wonderful things you are doing behind the scenes.
Then one day Lord you will come.
Thank you for your grace and peace that in the end
devours me, and brings me comfort.

Written when the shootings happened at the Sandy Hook Elementary School in Newton Connecticut. 12/14/2012

Heart and Mind

My mind holds thoughts of you,
all you have done for me.
My mind recalls how you died for **me,**
the pain you endured ...

My mind cannot comprehend the love you have for me,
how you loved me so much to die for me.

My heart keeps it all inside,
my heart holds those moments,
my heart is filled with thanksgiving,
for the things you have done for me.

My mind may one day forget.
My heart will always remember.

Lord Jesus

Loving of all
On earth was he
Rejoicing God's love, for all to see.
Destined to die, rejected by his own,
    he had to die to take his throne.

Just for us, he shed his blood
Ever to be with God above,
So that we all may someday see, his
Unending love, for you and me.
So much did God love everyone,
    he gave to us His only son.

Angel

I wish my angel
 I could see,
peeking lovingly at me.
So I could see that it is true
that God gave me an angel, too.

Grace

G*iven to us as a*
r*eminder, of*
a*ll the love Father God*
c*arries in his heart, for*
e*veryone.*

Reflection

*I reflect on the moments
You were silent in my life …
I see You in the midst of my pain.*

*You've conquered the evils that
surrounded me,
keeping me safe.*

*You are my savior, my King
in You alone I trust.*

*When I call Your name
You are there.
Thank you, Lord,
for being my friend and savior.*

Written when I was a teenager and someone tried to physically hurt me. I called out to Jesus and he rescued me.

Father's Love

Through the tears,
through the pains,
through the sorrows,
He remains.
nothing can separate His love from me,
my father, my father,
he loves me so much.

since the beginning of time,
He knew me by name,
I am not discouraged,
I am not ashamed.
for He, does not reject me,
because of my sins.
my father loves from within.

He holds me in the palm of His hand,
keeping me safe from harm.
He gives me shelter from the storms,
filling my heart with Joy.
He put his words in a book for me,
that I might know him, too.
His words will last forever,
even when the world is through.

Unanswered Prayer

Prayer's unanswered.
Love gone astray.
With every disappointment, a blessing.
His ways are always in your best interest.
He never thinks of himself.
Though everyone around you may leave you,
God never will.
He will always be with you,
no matter how much sorrow your heart might contain.
Be assured,
He is working a better way for you.
disappointments will become blessings

New Beginnings

Spring is upon us.
Birds are singing,
crows are calling,
flowers are pushing up
   through the soft earth.

   Sounds of children playing
remind me the cold
   has slithered away.

I caught a glimpse of a bird
 returning from her
winter home.
      She prepares a nest
   for her family.

I will provide for her,
as the Lord provides for me–
when I am weak from my flights.

I will watch her carry her babies
   on her back
   as she teaches them to fly.
I will rejoice with her
as the Lord rejoices with me.

*I will watch with sadness as
her babies enjoy their new found freedom.*

*They will look for their mother
gone from their sight,*

*will they meet again ...
will they know her?*

*Jesus will let go of us
so we may grow in him.
Will you seek him?
Or will you forget him?*

About the Author

Peggy is a devout Christian, wife, stepmother and Grandmother. Her strong faith in God is what made her the woman she is today. Her love for God is as unconditional as it is for her family and friends. She loves all life and is actively involved with animal shelters and has rescued several Rottweiler's over the years.

Peggy currently lives in Mahopac New York with her husband Joe of 28 years, they own World Homes Realty Located in Carmel, NY. She is also the owner of a very boisterous and verbal Parrot named Patti.

"May this book travel down many roads to many different homes, and never find a resting place on a shelf."

Please Review!

All independent authors depend upon reviews left on Amazon.com by their readers to help promote their books. Without these reviews, they will hardly get any notice. Please take the time to leave a short review. Simply go to Amazon.com, find the book and go to the book's page. Under the author's name will be a list of reviews and stars. Click here and there will be a big button saying "Create your own review". Please click here and review.

<u>Paste This link into your browser to review:</u>
http://www.amazon.com/review/create-review/ref=dpx_acr_rat_t2_wr_link?asin=0990389367

It only takes a minute!

Made in the USA
Lexington, KY
30 September 2014